Out of the Darkness

The
Theory of Everything

By
Marilyn Botterill

Produced by The Choir Press

ISBN 978-1-9160557-9-7

Copyright © Front and back cover designs
by Ebony Derham.

If you want to use any part of this publication,
please contact her via her email.
marilyn48@btopenworld.com

Contents

As It Should Have Been Told

Out of the Darkness

As It Should Have Been Told

Introduction

There have been challenges to conventional Christian religious belief and doctrine because of scientific discoveries and widespread education in the West which is extremely different from what used to be taught.

Religion contains some spiritual guidance but there is also a lot of dogma as well as rules and punishments that have been added over time. Religion is different from spirituality because it is man-made. Spirituality is the source.

Additionally what the Church told us the Bible says does not always hold up to what is actually written down in the Bible. Also because the understanding of the world and its beginnings were so different in the past it could only be perceived through the knowledge then available.

However, unfortunately, when repeated scientific evidence was put forward showing certain biblical teachings quite different from what appeared to be carefully assessed substantive data, the Church responded harshly. Now many people don't want to read the Bible and of those who do, there are broadly speaking, those who believe it implicitly and those who can't anymore but try to understand it in their own way. An impasse between some scientific understanding and Church doctrine developed and widened.

However as I understand what is written in the Bible, this period in our scientific understanding, science and traditional Christian teaching can be reconciled. Perhaps we humans needed to wait to this point in our history and development to see that and with a bit of luck those who fell away from believing in a God can have faith again. The misinformation or wrong telling starts with the creation story and Adam and Eve in the Garden of Eden.

It is not that the Church was deliberately wrong. Jesus was Jewish and the Creation Story was integral to Jewish belief. As a result, and because of it, it was important to the early Christians too. After all, it explained to them in a very different era of knowledge the beginning of the world. The story then became entrenched and parts reinterpreted by the Church Fathers after centuries of telling before science showed things were different. It is only in the recent historical past that such questions and conflicts of opinion started.

Chapter 1

The Church taught us that Adam and Eve were the first humans on earth; that God created Adam then Eve later from one of Adam's ribs after he was put into the Garden of Eden and couldn't find a help meet (partner or wife). They stayed there until God expelled them for being disobedient.

Science tells us that while our ancestors were on earth about 6 million years ago those who evolved into what many believe are our direct ancestors, Homo erectus, came about 200,000 years ago. Although periodic finds and ongoing research updates what is known, the information is consistently hundreds of thousands of years ago.

It has been calculated that Adam and Eve were created about 4,000 B.C.E.

The Church didn't know how to handle this massive difference and some very difficult situations resulted.

There are some Christians who still staunchly believe Adam and Eve were the first humans but many have made some compromises like it being symbolic. Others don't believe it at all.

However it is possible for scientific discoveries and the Bible to go hand in hand.

Adam and Eve were created but were not the first man and woman on earth and the Bible shows us this if the Bible is read without preconceived ideas. How and why they were created will follow after evidence from the King James Bible showing them not being the first people on earth.

After Adam and Eve were expelled from Eden, Eve gave birth to a son they called Cain and later a second son they called Able. When the boys were grown Cain murdered his brother Able because he was jealous of him and then ran away from home but he wasn't able to flee from "the Lord" who told him he was now cursed from the earth for what he had done and that he would be "a fugitive and vagabond for the rest of his life". Cain replied that this punishment was more than he could bear and was fearful that everyone who found him would kill him. Who was "everyone" outside of Eden? That's a statement expressing more people than just his parents whom he had run away from and at this point he doesn't have other siblings according to the Bible.

We are then told Cain went away from the Lord to the Land of Nod (a named place) which was east of Eden and lived there. Following that we are told he knew his wife making her pregnant. Where did this woman come from, the Land of Nod? The only woman mentioned before was Eve, his mother. We are also told that he built a city after his son was born and called it Enoch after the name he gave his son. Cities are cities because they contain a large group of people who are not family.

According to archaeologists, historians and scientists, cities started to be built around 4,500 B.C.E. with the City of Eridu in Mesopotamia being established first by the Sumerians. So cities were not new to the Middle and Near East having been built for about 500 years before the time we are told Adam and Eve were created.

The Bible seldom mentions female children. Women who are mentioned or have their names put down have a special or integral place in the story being told through the Bible. People questioning how Cain found this woman were told it was a daughter of Adam and Eve despite the fact the Bible doesn't state Adam and Eve had daughters until after having a third son when they were older. This was after Cain had got his wife. The fact 'daughters' were not mentioned until then infers that they hadn't had any earlier or else they would have been mentioned too, presumably important in this case as they were to help populate.

If Cain had married his sister as is the usual explanation for believers in the Creation story, something both church and state forbid us to do for genetic reasons, it would be considered incest. We are told he had no choice. So not only was he a murderer but also incestuous. Apparently though we are told he did not commit incest because there were no other women and God made us perfect despite the Bible telling us Cain was a murderer and Adam and Eve were expelled from Eden for disobedience to God by committing original sin. "Original sin" being disobedience to God although it has always had a sexual connotation, partly as least because we have been told by the Church that we are all born in sin because of what Adam and Eve did. Religious teaching has created many conundrums.

Chapter 2

Some biblical scholars say Genesis 1 chapter 1 and 2 are different versions of the same Creation Story with chapter 2 being more specific. All of what both say though was considered important enough to be kept. If this understanding is correct chapter 1 tells us that men and women were made to replenish the earth. That's men and women in the plural I believe, just as all the other creatures were made in the plural for the simple reason, God knew what he was doing. He created sufficient genetic diversity so as not to cause health problems within species as they reproduced.

We must also remember that these newly created people were blessed and told to replenish the earth. If you replenish something there has to be something similar before to replace. This is similar to Noah and his sons being blessed and told to replenish the earth by God after the Flood. We had been told before the Flood his sons had wives. In other words there's evidence in the Bible that Adam and Eve were not the only ones created and also evidence that there were people on the earth before any of those people created in Genesis 1 and 2 were created. Additionally, the Bible tells us there were gentiles. Who are the gentiles? Initially they were understood as being other nations; later they were specified as not being Jewish.

There is a difference though between the way the people are recorded in Genesis 1:1 and what we are told about Adam's creation. There is no record that the people made in Genesis 1:1 were told not to eat from the tree of the knowledge of good and evil or put into a garden called Eden. That was specific to Adam. While we are told those made in Genesis 1:1 were blessed and told to be fruitful and multiply and replenish the earth, and subdue it, we are not told Adam was told any of this. What we are told is that the Lord God "breathed into his nostrils the breath of life; and man became a living soul". However it is likely those made in chapter 1 were made in the way Adam was and also put into the Garden of Eden because of things told a little later in the Bible.

Finally language. Standardly until into the 19th century the word "man" could be used to mean a man, men or male and female depending on the context. If it was used to denote male and female it would be male and female in the plural like the word mankind which was used for a while but generally shortened to man. At a later date the word "mankind" was "revived" only to be discarded as it was considered too "sexist". However when it was used it was rather like how we use the word sheep. Although "ewe" is a word for a female sheep it is more common to just say sheep for male, female and plural. To demonstrate my point see Genesis 1 chapter 1 verse 26, "Let us make man - - : and let them have - - " using "man" as "mankind". This makes sense. Then in verse 27 of Genesis Chapter 1 there is an anomaly right in the middle of the sentence. "So God created man (mankind) in his own image (human form), but it goes on to say "- - in the image of God created he him;" but continues "male and female created he them." So is this said because God here is in male form and it was written and translated when men held control because we have been told before as well as in the next few words, that male and female were made by God?

In Genesis Chapter 2 we are told about Adam and "man" is used consistently in the singular to denote how he is made and calling him "the man" when he was told not to eat from the tree of the knowledge of good and evil. We are also told he was alone, without a help meet (female partner) yet we have been told in Chapter 1 God made male and female to replenish the earth after he had made all the creatures. Adam being alone could simply mean that he had no partner.

Society was male oriented and the Church taught Adam and Eve were the first humans with Eve being made from one of Adam's ribs making Adam the first human but it was an inherited belief.

Chapter 3

The first parts of the Bible were passed down by word of mouth for at least centuries but most probably thousands of years before being written down. The oldest piece of manuscript so far found containing part of the Genesis Creation story dates between 100 BCE and 1 BCE. It was found amongst the Dead Sea scrolls. Some researchers suggest that older copies of Genesis may have been written down as early as the 8th century BCE because Hebrew letters and writing were starting to be standardised then. The original Hebrew writing was pictographic like Egyptian hieroglyphs and also like ancient Egyptian there were no vowels. A big difference though was that ancient Hebrew had 22 pictures while ancient Egyptian had about 700 which increased to about 5,000 in the Greco/Roman period. ("about" because specialists do not agree to the exact number) We are told that each Hebrew pictograph had multiple meanings and the meaning depended on its context which would make it understood quite precisely. At this time the Hebrews lived a simple pastoral life so there was no need for a complicated written language. However over time it was developed, and by and /or during the Babylonian captivity period it had become a new script developed from the pictographs but strongly influenced by the Canaanite/Phoenician written language. It is called Proto or Paleo Hebrew and was the beginning of the change towards the distinctive square shaped Hebrew writing.

If there are copies of the Creation Story from this time that haven't been found yet or been destroyed by time there is still a period of about 4,000 years between Adam and Eve's creation and the writing we know about. Stories told rather than read can have a little change here or there to emphasise a point or make a situation clearer to the audience listening. It has always been that way. This would have also been the case if the storyteller was using the pictographs as a guide. Also there would have been many groups being told independent of each other and that would mean many tellers. Different people don't tend to tell the same story in exactly the same way even if they keep to the same main points. An example is the Gospels in the New Testament. Even the same person doesn't usually tell the same story in exactly the same way multiple times. These are some of the reasons for writing down information.

Another important consideration is that language changes over time. In one lifetime the meaning of a word can change totally. For example the very controversial meaning behind the word "gay" which now means sexually attracted to the same sex simply meant "to be happy". Another word out of hundreds that have totally changed their meaning over time is "nice". It came from a Greek word meaning ignorant then in the 14th century it came to mean foolish or silly. Going on to the 18th century it was used to describe extravagance, ostentation and wantonness which were often directly or indirectly admired. From then "nice" came to be used to describe people or things people liked.

Words are there to express and explain. As time goes on perception of the environment and life changes gradually and subtly or momentously when things like war or an invention to make life easier or more enjoyable happens. Words evolve to express what people want to say.

Go back to Charles Dickens' English and you can see quite a different way of expressing yourself because life was quite different. Many common words to us now were not in existence then and vice versa. They would not have known what we meant if we spoke of a phone, a fridge, a computer or an aeroplane for example and how we phrase our sentences and address people are also totally different. Do we use the phrase "cop a mouse" (get a black eye) now or know what a cashmarie (fish seller) is? People walked or went by cart, carriage or horse. Now go back 500 more years to William Shakespeare's English which is very different again and you might need a little help to understand some. That is only half of 1,000 years from Dickens. If you go back from Shakespeare's time about another 100 years or four more generations to Chaucer's and the English he used, it is extremely different in every way. You would need to learn it or get help to understand what was being said because the grammar, spelling and many of the words were so different and that still isn't even going back 1,000 years from Dickens. If there were copies of Genesis written in the 8th century B.C.E. there was still a period of well over 3,000 years between the first telling of the Genesis Creation Story and the time it might first have been written down.

Chapter 4

As stated, language is there to express oneself in life. Words and society evolve hand in hand. Everything around us changes over time from occupations to the way we travel, from the food we eat and the clothes we wear to the homes we live in. Some occupations from even the recent past and commonly done things which were part of everyday life are no longer done or done in a totally different way. Farming for example, which had been a major employer of casual and manual labour for hundreds of years, became increasingly mechanised during the 20th century. The same has happened to the craft skills like furniture making, clothes making and making pottery for our plates and mugs etc. Only a century earlier the Industrial Revolution began this movement from work by hand often in the maker's home to work by machine in a "factory".

Development goes forward and backwards. There were some ancient civilisations, specifically Bronze Age Mohenjo-Daro which is currently in Pakistan, and Minoan Crete, which had piped water and toilets in everyone's home. Later the Roman Empire brought plumbing to their empire. However when their empire declined and collapsed plumbing also went. It wasn't until into the 20th century that people started to have running water into their homes again, usually just one tap which would give cold water and no indoor toilet or bath. There might be an outside toilet, really a glorified hole, no plumbing. There may be a seat over it and a little shed around it but some earth, ash or sand had to be sprinkled in after using.

Food was seasonal and mostly locally produced until after World War II when it became increasingly more diverse because imported and "luxury" items of all sorts became far more available. More and varied shops came about to supply demand which steadily increased and then came the "supermarket".

Words "die out" from lack of use or get invented or changed to accommodate a new thing like "supermarket" and "electricity". There are many more created words and ones that change with the times like the word "buggy" for transporting infants when before that a "pram" was used. A pram was originally called a "perambulator" because the person who pushed it walked or "perambulated" – another word that has gone out of use. Now what relationship do the words "perambulator" and "buggy" have to each other? The only connection is the meaning. The same happened with some words in the Bible. Firstly this happened while it was being passed down by word of mouth and secondly when it was frozen in time after being canonised.

A key example and a word necessary to clarify is the word "serpent" in the Garden of Eden. To us it is a synonym for snake. In ancient Hebrew pictographs there was a symbol that while now is more commonly interpreted as seed with variants including heir, life and fish has also been interpreted as serpent or snake. This pictograph called "nun" is a small oval shape with a wiggly "tail" coming from it. If taken as serpent or snake, understood in context could mean adversary. I am taking it to mean that because it makes sense of Adam and Eve's story if you want to understand their story realistically as you can the creation of our world. It also makes sense of what is said a little further on in Genesis too.

Going on in time quickly, to the Proto/Paleo Hebrew writing, many consider the evolution of the "nun" symbol to mean sorcery and magic so we have a "snake" (adversary) becoming Satan or the Devil in disguise.

Even with a far greater vocabulary today we have many words with multiple and often unconnected, very different meanings like the words "file", "mouse" and "bark".

The story of Cain killing his brother has influenced listeners and readers of the story. Cain is thought to be evil and linked with the Devil, not the son of Adam.

So there was an adversary to the Lord in the Garden of Eden.

Chapter 5

We are told Adam and Eve were made. Step by step consider these points told by the Bible in Chapter 1 of Genesis 1 very carefully and with no preconceived ideas. Take what is being said as if this was the very first time you read it or heard of it. Although there are many translations I am using the King James Bible version for quotes.

The bold opening statement "In the beginning God created the heaven and the earth" – exactly as it says – In the beginning God (as Creator) made the heaven (what is beyond Earth's atmosphere) and the Earth.

Most scientists agree that Earth and our solar system started from the "Big Bang", that is, the universe began in a sudden and so far unexplained event which has been called the "Big Bang" because it was a massive explosion of energy. Energy remained and matter began to form.

Then we are told in the Bible "The world was without form, and void;" – in other words there were the elements to form or make our world but they hadn't done it at this point – so we are at the very beginning. The Bible continues "and darkness was upon the face of the deep". Deep space is dark and after the Big Bang scientists agree that there was total darkness initially. This was caused by the huge number of particles in the atmosphere from the Big Bang which blocked the light from the explosion.

The Bible then tells us that "the Spirit of God moved upon the face of the waters". NASA has found water and water vapour in space. The largest amount of water so far found in space surrounds a huge "feeding" black hole or quasar and it seems the black hole/ quasar is making it although scientists can't explain why. After Albert Einstein theorised about black holes there has been periodic scientific interest in them and they were found to exist. More study has been done by several astro-physicists including Stephen Hawking and we now know that they are extremely dense and can gravitationally pull in anything that gets too close to them which makes them increase in size. These astro-physicists have theorised about white holes, the opposite of black holes. White holes would expel anything they contain and push away anything that came too close. I suggested in my book "Out of the Darkness, the Theory of Everything" (now re-published by Marilyn Botterill) that not only does a black hole invert when full, not being able to expand anymore, it becomes a white hole and that was how our universe/ solar system began. The Big Bang was a black hole inverting, becoming a white hole spewing out its contents. I also suggest that the water NASA has found being made by and surrounding a large black hole could be there not only to control the heat of the explosion/inversion whenever it happens but for use on a planet/ the planets to be. In this case the scientists state that around that black hole/ quasar there is the equivalent to 140 trillion (U.S.) times the amount of water that we have in all of the oceans of the world.

After being told the Spirit of God moved upon the face of the waters we are told "God said, Let there be light: and there was light - - and God divided the light from the darkness." Scientists say that after the complete darkness following the Big Bang, light appeared. This was because the particles within the atmosphere from the Big Bang started to reform becoming the first stars and planets clearing space sufficiently for light still coming from the explosion to shine through. And God called the light Day and the darkness he called Night."

Then God said,

"Let there be a firmament in the midst of the waters, and let it divide the waters from the waters. - - . And God called the firmament Heaven."

In other words the atmosphere and heavens were made. Even now to look up to the heavens or heavenward means to look up to the sky and includes what is in it.

Then he said,

"Let the waters under the heaven be gathered together unto one place, and let the dry land appear: and it was so. And God called the dry land Earth: and the gathering together of the waters called he Seas: -".

Scientists not only agree that our Earth and solar system were made next but that there was originally just one land mass on the Earth which was totally surrounded by sea. That land mass has been called Pangea. It is over millennia that the single land mass broke into pieces and became continents and islands because of what is called the continental drift.

Then we are told "let the earth bring forth grass, the herb yielding seed and the fruit tree - - " This is the order of the specified vegetation on earth though scientists believe moss came before grass and bushes before trees.

We are told next in the Bible,
"Let there be lights in the firmament of the heaven to divide the day from the night; - - -. And God made two great lights; the greater light to rule the day, and the lesser light to rule the night: he made the stars also. And God set them in the firmament of the heaven to give light upon the earth, - -."
Scientists tell us that the sun was made before our Earth and the moon after. The Bible tells us that God made two great lights and that the greater light ruled the day and the lesser light the night. It does not state when they were made.

According to scientists life on Earth began in the sea. The Bible states
"And God said, Let the waters bring forth abundantly the moving creature that hath life, and fowl that may fly above the earth - -".
Then we are told again with a little more detail,
"And God created whales, and every living creature that moveth, which the water brought forth abundantly, after their kind, and every winged fowl after his kind: - - "
I believe these statements include the creatures that came from the sea to land and started evolving and developing to live on land. It is just

very simply and straightforwardly put down, : "let the waters bring forth abundantly the moving creature that hath life" and again after God created the whales he created "every living creature that the waters brought forth".

These are generic statements but affirm that God made all creatures and that life came from the water whether it stayed in the water or came to land and adapted to live on land. Interestingly science has now found that whales came from the water, (sea), developed as mammals on land and then returned to the sea. Is this why whales are the only specifically named creature? Additionally science has now acknowledged that what it thought was a clear-cut pattern of evolution of the creatures is not so clear cut.

Finally man or mankind (humankind) was made both male and female which is also correct from a scientific perspective. Everything made was in the plural because God wanted the genetic diversity necessary for healthy reproduction.

Chapter 6

According to Genesis 1:1 the people made were to be vegan and care for God's creation. God wanted his creation nurtured, not killed or damaged and made food for this to be possible. We are not told specifically that Adam was told to be vegan but he and his descendants through to Noah probably were because we are told after the Flood permission was given for meat to be eaten although there were conditions. (Genesis chapter 9 verses 2 – 4). This could be added to the evidence that Adam was one of the people made in the first chapter of Genesis. He was then individualised in the second chapter when we are told he was alone, i.e. he didn't have a partner. Then we are told how one was made for him who became known as Eve. It was the Church that emphatically told us they were the first people on Earth. As said before this was an inherited belief. We are also told that God had completed his work and rested on the seventh day of creation and sanctified (blessed) it. For this reason we have traditionally had Sunday as a rest day every week but life changes and there are now many variations of shift work and other distractions. The other Abrahamic religions have a different "seventh day / rest day". Jewish people have theirs on a Saturday and Moslems chose Friday. Each religion wanted to be different.

The second chapter of Genesis actually begins with a recapitulation,

"Thus the heavens and the earth were finished and all the host of them"

With a little more three verses on,

"These are the generations of the heavens and of the earth when they were created, in the day that the Lord God made the earth and the heavens, and every plant of the field before it was in the earth and every herb of the field before it grew –"

Recapping what had been said in a story before continuing was standard practice in early Near Eastern writing. It is called by a Hebrew name "toledoth". The recapping ends when it states there was no-one to till the ground. The recap was meant to lead on to the next part of the story which in this case was the Bible saying there was no-one to till the ground. It isn't saying no humans were on the earth. Tilling the ground requires a plough. Ploughs were not invented until the Sumerians about 3,000 B.C.E. that is 1,000 years after Adam and Eve were created. About another 1,000 years further on nearer our time, the Egyptians made some good improvements on this design which had great effect on their crops. That was about 2,000 years after Adam and Eve were created then expelled from Eden. Adam had to cultivate using something very much more primitive and laborious like a sharpened stick. He was told "In the sweat of thy face shalt thou eat bread" as he was "to till the ground from whence he was taken" the words of the story probably "updated" after ploughs were invented and as the story was passed on orally this was not difficult to do. Also it is not until more recent times that history has been understood with far more perspective and detail. This is so eloquently shown in paintings painted in the Middle Ages which frequently show people from Biblical times dressed similarly to the artist's contemporaries.

Adam's punishment was made to sound and be understood as a terrible punishment. It certainly would have been really hard work to "scratch" the soil with a sharpened stick to release the nutrients to enable him to feed himself and his family. Countless generations though have believed that that statement supported the Church telling us Adam and Eve were the first humans and it was used like that. However we have not been told there were no other humans, in fact we were told in the previous chapter of the Bible men and women were created to replenish the earth. Also we are not told in the Bible, Adam and Eve were the first people on earth - anywhere. Even Jesus' well known quoted response about the first humans on earth could be understood both ways and still be correct. Gospel of Matthew, Chapter 19, verse 4,

"Have ye not read, that he which made them at the beginning made them male and female."

We are just told there was no-one to till the ground. So why do we have two people singled out who have the names Adam and Eve?

Chapter 7

After a little way into reading the Bible it becomes increasingly obvious we are following certain members of Adam and Eve's family. Initially we are told about Cain's descendants and that five generations from Cain, Lamech murdered two men which could be another indication there were other people around because the victims were not named as family as Able was.

We are then told Adam and Eve had another son they called Seth. Eve said he was from God to replace Abel and he proved Godly. A new chapter (Genesis chapter 5) starts, opening with the words, "This is the book of the generations of Adam. In the day that God created man, in the likeness of God made he him. Male and female created he them; and blessed them, and called their name Adam, in the day when they were created".
Adam and Eve wanted to start afresh with Seth so repeat, in abridged form, the Creation Story.

Eve is not mentioned by name here because lineages in the Bible were recorded through the male line only. Also we had been told earlier that because Adam was alone Eve was made from one of his ribs. However from the way this toledoth is worded it seems as if verse 26 of Genesis 1:1 is virtually copied and important. It also suggests Adam was one of the men made in the Genesis 1:1 group who were to "replenish the earth".

We are told he was made in the likeness of God and that male and female were made and they were blessed which comes from Genesis 1:1 and not how Adam or Eve's creation is recorded in Genesis 1:2.

God made man, that is mankind because it doesn't say "the man". Adam is then putting himself forward as being made in the image of God. He was made and resembled in appearance who made him. Then we are told that male and female were made, amplifying the statement "God made man" that is, God made mankind.

The men and women created in Chapter 1 could have been made in exactly the same way as we are told Adam was in chapter 2 – out of the elements of the earth.

Going back to this toledoth, male and female created humans are called Adam! So it is understandable that Biblical scholars have said that Genesis chapter 2 gives more detail. However, this detail hones in to one man's dilemma of not finding a partner when we have been told male and female had already been made and God was pleased with his work and rested. In chapter 2, Adam is alone and God makes him a "help meet" (Eve). After that Adam and Eve become one – had a sexual relationship - and then a little later they eat the fruit Adam had been told not to. We only follow their story at this point, not the other created people although they seem to be mentioned a little later in the Bible.

Adam and Eve get expelled from Eden for eating the fruit of the forbidden tree. They have three sons we are told about. After the third son, Seth, we are told that "this is the book of the generations of Adam". What follows is a selected lineage of Adam's descendants through Seth and the times and events surrounding them although we are also told Adam and Eve had sons and daughters after having him. The Bible, literally meaning "the book(s)" as both Greek and Latin roots of the word agree, continues to follow the lives and times of selected descendants of Seth until and then after the creation of the Jewish nation. For Christians who follow Jesus we learn later that He is a descendent of Shem, a son of Noah. The Bible's New Testament is the story of Jesus.

Going back to the toledoth previously mentioned seems to strengthen the case that Adam and Eve were not the only people created. No reason is given in the Bible why Adam didn't have a partner/wife originally but Jewish folklore tells us that he had a first wife called Lilith from the people made in Genesis 1:1. However a great deal of controversy ended up surrounding this understanding.

As stated earlier when reading "man", "mankind" or humankind can be substituted for modern readers. The word "man" used in this context is again generic and plural. It is also not gender specific. We are told that humans were made, seemingly in the plural, just as all his other creatures were made in the plural and I repeat that was for genetic reasons. Humans there though were told to replenish the earth. In this recap when we are told male and female were created we are told "they" were called Adam which is giving male and female the same generic name. Interestingly the Hebrew for Adam means "to be red in colour" and the Hebrew "Adamah" means "earth" while in the Akkadian language which influenced early Hebrew writing it means "to make". So it seems all these people were made in the same way the Adam we know was? Also although there are clays of different colours "red" (a reddish brown) is one of them and some translations say that Adam was made from clay. So this toledoth, which as usual is very condensed, is also giving some new information with the recapped information. It tells us men and women were made as Adam was, "out of the earth" or as some translate, out of "clay". Then we are told the people made were called Adam which is new although the Adam we know has taken or been given this name. Note Eve was not made in this way although women were made.

Traditional Jewish belief says that Adam and Eve were the first people on earth. Abraham, the progenitor of the Jewish nation was a direct descendent of Adam and Eve through Seth. It is because their story was copied and included lock, stock and barrel into Christianity before humans knew any different about the origin of the world that Christians were taught the same.

The great importance attached to the Jewish story though is how they came to believe in One God, the Creator of Heaven and Earth and try to follow a Godly life. They are the leaders of the three monotheistic religions. First came Judaism, next came Christianity and then more recent in time of establishment came Islam whose followers believe Mohammed (peace be upon him) was the last prophet.

Adam and Eve's lineage continued and was recorded through sons as was the custom. When it got to Noah and his sons Shem, Ham and Japheth, more was said because Noah believed in God and tried to live a Godly life while people around him did not care about God and living as God wanted. We are told that for this reason God sent a great flood. Noah was warned by God and built a boat (the Ark) to keep his family safe and with them he took pairs of animals he had been told to save too. Noah's sons were mentioned by name because they were considered important to this family line. They were male and were to re-populate the world with their wives; that is their world or rather their area and keep their family line going after the Flood. "And God blessed Noah, and his sons, and said unto them, Be fruitful and multiply, and replenish the earth." This is the same statement that is used in the Genesis creation story and used for the same reason. It was to keep the knowledge of God alive and to pass on a better way to live just as it had been planned when people were made and put into Eden.

To have actually experienced this flood must have seemed that the whole world was flooded. Anyone caught up in a cataclysmic event can't imagine anywhere that hasn't been affected. Shem, one of Noah's sons was a forbear of Jesus, and the Old Testament, which starts with the creation of the world and everything in it, continues following the ups and downs of the emerging Jewish race. Traditionally this has been important to Christians because it gives the background to Jesus who was Jewish and it was believed by them Adam and Eve were the first people on Earth.

Chapter 8

As a prelude to Adam being created we are told a mist went up from the earth and watered the whole face of the ground. Mists do wet the ground and while in the air make seeing difficult. The Lord God could come out of the mist being discreet, especially if there were other "evolved" humans about. He knew what He wanted to do, form man out of the "dust of the earth". This could have been some form of genetic engineering and He wouldn't want "evolved" man to see what He was doing.

Why did He want to do this? It seems that He was making a group of people, not just Adam, to go out into the world with certain knowledge and a better way to live. There appears evidence in the Bible to prove this. What was hoped for "in the beginning" hadn't worked out. The first people on earth were not vegan as God had wanted (Genesis 1 verse 29) and they did not care about the world and His creation. There was exploitation of people and resources. There were wars and great cruelty to humans and animals. There was a lot of wickedness. (Genesis chapter 6 verse 5)

The reason for the people being made in Genesis 1 chapter 1 was an attempt to redirect the people of earth to live in the way God had wanted when He created our world. He wanted them to "be fruitful and multiply" so they could "replenish the Earth" that is, to be able to replace the existing order which was "evil". To refill the world with people knowing what he was teaching them in Genesis chapter 1. These newly made people were to "subdue it", that is, to lead the people already on the Earth and bring them under control using the knowledge they were given. If these created people had children and intermarried with those outside and passed on the knowledge they had been given they could set an example and also try to teach "evolved" humans to live in peace and with care to all of the natural world. The created humans were also instructed to have "dominion" over "the fish of the sea", "the fowl of the air" and "every living thing that moveth upon the earth," The word "dominion" built on the Latin word "domus" (private family house or home) , originally meant the lord or master of the house. So God wanted all his creatures looked after as if they belonged to someone's family. God would have meant a good, caring family.

All God's initial creation had been made in plural and it becomes increasingly clear the Old Testament develops into a story about a specific lineage and their times. Adam and Eve had made a big mistake and were expelled from Eden and not allowed back in. Protection was put in place to prevent them from returning, Genesis Chapter 3 verse 24:-

"he placed at the east of the garden of Eden Cherubims and a flaming sword which turned every way, to keep the way of the tree of life."

I suggest "The Tree of Life" is the project. This protection doesn't seem to have been there before Adam and Eve ate from "the Tree of Knowledge of Good and Evil". Not only did it prevent Adam and Eve from returning it prevented any more "outsiders" (adversaries) to the "The Tree of Life" from entering.

There is a passage a little further on in Genesis, at the beginning of chapter 6, which has also caused puzzlement. It says:
"And it came to pass, when men (mankind / humans) began to multiply on the face of the earth and daughters were born unto them, That the sons of God saw the daughters of men that they were fair; and they took them wives of all which they chose."
I suggest these "sons of God" were from Eden, descended from those who were made in Genesis 1:1. However Genesis Chapter 6 continues,
"And the Lord had said, My spirit shall not always

strive with man, for that he also is flesh _".
(Christians believe "the Lord" in Eden is Jesus in flesh at this point). He (the Lord) representing God, hoped things would get better; He wanted things to get better. These men were made with the plan that they go out and intermarry with women already out there in the hopes of improving the human outlook, understanding and behaviour. In fact the Bible goes on to say:

"when the Sons of God came in unto the daughters of men, and they bare children to them, the same became mighty men which were of old, men of renown."

The plan seemed to work although the Bible, because it is the Bible talking, only speaks of male descendants. However the descendants pleased Him. It must also be remembered that at this time and place historically women's position in society was moving from a position equal to men to a position lower than men.

The Bible continues that despite mighty men of renown being born, God saw there was still a lot of wickedness on the earth because many humans' thoughts were continually evil. In context one of the things he was not happy with was the reduced status of women. Originally man and woman were made to be equal, to balance each other, to be partners in life just as Adam and Eve had been at first. It was only after Eve then Adam were tempted and succumbed that Eve was told she was to have him rule over her. That was specific to Eve for what she had done. It was not stated that all women should be ruled over. That was the Church Fathers interpretation of the Creation Story and people could not gainsay what the Church taught. For centuries ordinary people were not allowed to read the Bible even if they had learnt to read.

So what had Eve done? She tempted Adam to eat the fruit of the forbidden tree, the tree that it is recorded Adam was told not to eat from. There is no record of Eve being told not to eat from it. However both were punished and banished from Eden. Eve's punishment was all linked with sex. She would have great sorrow conceiving and bearing children. This was/is often understood as pain in childbirth and pregnancies being difficult. She would also have more children than the original plan. Additionally she would only have desire for her husband and he would rule over her. The Church Fathers put forward all women were potential temptresses and needed supervision by a male generally understood as their father then their husband. This punishment was only meted out to Eve – "Unto the woman - - " not unto women! But it was interpreted by the Church Fathers when society was male dominant and unfortunately many women do suffer with difficult pregnancies and births so they thought it fitted or wanted it to fit.

Though not specified in the Bible it is apparent that the real reason Adam and Eve were expelled from Eden and not allowed back in was because Eve, then Adam, had a sexual relationship with someone from outside Eden and Cain was the result of Eve doing this although she had a sexual relationship with Adam when they were outside Eden and before the child (Cain) was born.

We are told in the Bible she was tempted to eat from the tree of the knowledge of good and evil by a talking serpent whom religion has said was the Devil in disguise. However not only was there a pictograph in the Hebrews first written language that could be interpreted as serpent/ snake/adversary, but there have historically been so many sexual inferences around this story and a general understanding or belief that the serpent was the Devil in disguise. This was not only because of how Cain turned out but because people know women can't get pregnant from snakes. And why was she told she would only have desire for her husband listed as part of her punishment? It seems she might have lost it to this "outsider", the "adversary" to God's plan.

Additionally after their encounter, Adam and Eve were aware they were naked or they knew what they had done was seen by the Lord. The Bible tells us that the Lord spoke to the serpent and put a curse on him so the Lord had seen what happened. Before they were expelled clothes of skins were made for them, presumably to help them fit in with the people outside. Bear in mind historically not all peoples wore clothes and some only wore them as protection to the elements. To these people nakedness was not sinful or embarrassing but normal. However, another meaning of being naked is that someone can see through another's deceit.

After Adam and Eve were expelled protection was put in place around Eden to prevent further disruption to the plan.

As shown earlier Adam and Eve were not the first people on Earth. They were among a group made for a special purpose; that was, to redirect the way humans were going. I suggest the Tree of Knowledge of good and evil was a euphemism for people outside Eden. Therefore eating the fruit was a euphemism for having a relationship with someone from outside Eden and Adam was told this because he hadn't found a woman in Eden he wanted to be with. After Eve had succumbed to temptation, having a sexual relationship with someone from outside Eden, Adam was tempted, but men do not get pregnant. So although they both seemed to have had sexual relationships with people they were not meant to, Eve became pregnant as a result.

As time went by, after Christianity's emergence, it started to become an organized, international religion with a central administration and statements of belief. Among these was the Doctrine of Original Sin started by Irenaeus the Bishop of Lyons in the 2nd century C.E. It states that we are all conceived and then born in sin because of what Adam and Eve did which is another and very pointed sexual reference to what they did do, but now called "Original Sin" by the Church.

To help redeem babies the Church stipulated they were to be baptised or christened as soon after birth as possible to prevent them from going to Hell and being with the Devil if they died. Infant mortality was extremely high. Traditionally if a baby cried when the holy water was sprinkled on its forehead during a baptism it was said to be a good sign as the devil had jumped out.

Jewish people do not follow this doctrine and

neither did the first Christians although the latter baptised. This was for washing away the sins of the past and starting a new life as a Christian. Also Jewish people blame Adam as much as Eve for the "fall from grace", being expelled from Eden.

Chapter 9

Notice there has been a differentiation made between God and what God does and the Lord God or the Lord with also a mention of the Spirit of God. God has the ultimate power and the Lord God or the Lord works with Him and for Him with power given to Him from God through the Holy Spirit. God as the Creator of all could not be limited to a human body. Jesus, as Christians understand the person in Eden was, is the link.

Jesus created through God. That's the "us" in Genesis 1. Jesus was in human form to be able to live on the earth. It is He who walked in the Garden of Eden and again created through God and it was He who spoke to Cain after he'd murdered Able. Even Jesus says in the New Testament "before the world I am" and "I am one with my Father." He also shows us that He could come back to life after being killed – to show us there is life after earthly death.

Out of Eden, Adam and Eve and their descendants copied some of the customs and traditions of those outside. It was a very hierarchical world. For that reason and because he was not given a name in the Creation Story we have Jesus being called Lord.

Time. There is/has been so much argument about what a day actually meant regarding God creating our universe in the 6 days stated in the Bible. Was it an actual day as we know it or 1,000 years as it is spoken of in the Bible (2 Peter 3:8) when a day to the Lord is like a thousand years. Does it really matter? God created. That is surely the important bit. "Trust in the Lord thy God" – He knows best. Leave it, don't argue, follow the good teachings instead. The length of time involved is a point of interest nothing more. He did it in his own time. Don't be like scholars in the Middle Ages who had a popular debate to argue how many angels could dance on a pin head. What really matters is living right. The Hebrew word "yom" is another word that has different meanings and should be understood in context. It could mean sunrise to sunset within a 24 hour period, a literal day, or an unspecified period of time like "the day of - - " meaning an "age" or large time period. What really matters, or should matter to us, is that we look after His creation, the natural world, in all its diversity. That is what God wants and has always wanted. Genesis Chapter 1 verse 26. But again this has been overlooked or misunderstood. God wanted the humans he created in Genesis to look after his creation. As part of this looking after he wanted them and his creatures to be vegan and provided food for this to happen. Genesis Chapter

1 verses 29 and 30. What we should be discussing are the best ways to look after his creation/ our world, and then we would have a beautiful, balanced and sustainable ecosystem and be healthier and less stressed

Chapter 10

Christians who follow(ed) Jesus, who was a Jew, inherited or "took on" quite a bit of the Jewish scripture including what they have in their Torah. This, put together, became the Christians "Old Testament".

However, also integral to the Jewish background is Jewish folklore and a system used by Jewish rabbis called Midrash. Midrash, specifically the form called Aggadah, is a way of explaining what seem to be inconsistencies in scripture. The "Great Midrash" is the name of the collections linked to the five books of the Torah which for Christians starts with the Book of Genesis, the first book of the Old Testament. Although most Midrashim were compiled between about 200 and 1000 C.E. and did not really affect what the Christians had acquired, many Midrashim circulated orally before then because the scriptures had been passed on orally for much of that time.

The Jewish teachers had a way of being able to explain their scripture with relevance to the people they were talking to. This could mean slight variations to the way the stories were told with certain words or phrases adapted for clearer understanding. There were many groups and many rabbis. These biblical scholars knew times changed and wanted to make their story relevant. As said before, words together with their understanding can change over time and fixed script does not.

One of the stories told which became part of Jewish folklore was that Adam had a wife before Eve. She was from the people we are told God created in Chapter 1 of Genesis 1. I am stating this because it seems that at one point it was realised that Adam was not the first or only person on earth. He was the first man of their special family. Anyway the story goes that this first wife called Lilith was not happy being with Adam because she did not want to be subservient to him, specifically, to lie under him during sex. She wanted to be his equal in everything.

The story of Adam's first wife continued in Jewish folklore and Lilith became demonised and blamed among other things for taking babies' lives while they were asleep. In other words she caused "cot deaths".

It was quite common at that time and even today not unknown for fruit to be used as euphemisms or synonyms for sex. The people outside Eden had knowledge of good and evil with often evil predominating as we have been told. In other words Adam was told specifically that he could have contact and interaction or a relationship with anyone in Eden but with no-one from outside. Genesis 1 chapter 2 verses 16 and 17 euphemises it. However as he didn't find anyone God made him a partner.

Going back to Eve, this adversary in the Garden of Eden was someone from outside who had managed to entice her or "tempt" her to have a sexual relationship with him. She succumbed; found it enjoyable and tempted Adam to do the same. They had become worldly by mixing with people from outside Eden and were expelled from Eden for it and prevented from getting back in by protection put there. This also prevented any other people from outside Eden getting into Eden so the rest of the group could finish learning what the Lord intended them to know. Also there would not be another pregnancy created by a man from outside Eden. Eve gave birth to Cain who certainly was not an example of goodness. She said he was a child from the Lord. Religion tells us that the serpent was the Devil or Satan in disguise. It shows there must have been some realisation that Eve had not born Adam's son and as previously said, "Lord" was a deferential title outside Eden to a male. Adam and Eve's maker at this point then became "Lord God". The events were spoken about and passed on outside Eden. And the person who made her pregnant was from outside Eden.

So this "adversary" in the Garden of Eden, the someone (or more) who shouldn't have been there, has been described in veiled terms over millennia for different reasons. This includes as a snake or serpent but a woman cannot be made pregnant by a snake or serpent.

There's a Jewish story that says Cain, Eve's first born son, was actually the son of Eve and Satan, "personifying" the "adversary" in Eden. It makes sense that Cain wasn't Adam's son.

The command not to eat from the tree of knowledge of good and evil seems to be a euphemism for mixing with people from outside Eden. It didn't kill Adam and Eve but it did stop them being part of the project for which they and others were made. It messed things up badly for Adam and Eve and for everyone following their story literally.

Adam and Eve knew they had done wrong. They were no longer innocent and realised they could not be part of the plan. They were embarrassed, afraid and tried to hide but the Lord who must have seen exactly what they had done because he saw the serpent (intruder) and cursed "him",

 "- - upon thy belly shalt thou go and dust shalt thou eat - - ".

This was a standard curse of the time to a person who had done you great wrong. It did not change a walking serpent/snake into a crawling one.

Adam and Eve having a sexual relationship with someone outside of God's plan was "original sin". It related to them alone not as the church fathers put forward that we are all born in sin because of what they did. Sexual relationships are not sinful. God had made all his creatures sexual and blessed them.

Possibly Adam and Eve didn't understand the implications of what they had done until afterwards but their descendants certainly tried to atone for it and ingrain in their children a belief in One God.

Even logically it is questionable that we are all born in sin because conception of a new human is through the joining of a sperm and ovum, something God blessed. The only way out of this was to say sex was sinful and for procreation only. It should not be enjoyed, and it should only be had on certain days and in certain ways. These restrictions on a married couple's relationship were rigidly enforced as punishable offences. Also sexual relationships outside marriage were considered heinous and severely punished and stigmatised. Yet God blessed all living creatures including mankind to make them sexual and did not put any restrictions on it. Some early societies did though like the Sumerians and Egyptians then later Moses with one of the 10 Commandments, "thou shalt not commit adultery".

This was done to keep order in the society and try to prevent the suffering adultery could cause.

Chapter 11

Although Christianity became a religion distinct from Judaism during the later Roman period it went through quite a few major changes between then and when the Bible was canonised in the latter part of the 4th century C.E. Even then the canonisation went through "stages" and different churches had a different "canon" although the majority of the parts within were the same. Then came the schisms, bloodshed and development of heresy trials with torture and death penalties for those not believing exactly as the establishing church taught. It taught there could be no variants.

Historically magic and superstition were part of many peoples' lives. When people can't understand anything rationally they try to understand it in other ways. The Church called those things it taught that couldn't be understood rationally like the Eucharist bread and wine becoming Jesus' flesh and blood during the service, "mysteries". Everything that didn't fit into their categorising of mysteries became increasingly suspect.

Life was very harsh and unpredictable. Death was commonplace. A bad harvest caused starvation and the possibility of death. Infection and disease frequently followed an accident because hygiene was not properly understood and this caused the likelihood of dying. Childbirth was so potentially dangerous for both the woman giving birth and the baby that the woman was required to have left a Will if she had possessions. Illnesses were often fatal too and when the Bubonic Plague or "Black Death" came in the mid 1300's it was believed the end of the world was near. All this was believed to be not just God's judgement but coming from the Devil. The church tried to help but because it had developed "mysteries" of its own it had only made people more superstitious and things that went bad became blamed on the Devil. The Devil personified bad luck and misfortune and had become someone very real to them. Paintings on Church walls and in religious works of art often depicted the Devil or Satan to remind people that if they did not do as instructed by the Church they would go to Hell when they died and be punished by the Devil (Satan) and his helpers. By the Middle Ages everything that was bad was likely to be called the work of the Devil. Hence it was accepted that the "serpent" in the Garden of Eden was the Devil in disguise.

Jumping to the 20th century, language, especially written language, became increasingly less descriptive beyond what was essential for the story. Not only had the pace of life begun to increase but leisure time gained competitors. Radio, films and television were invented, then expanding social media platforms and outings, holidays and visits to places that were once out of reach to most people or newly created like theme parks. Before all this stories and storytelling were a main form of entertainment and life was still largely based around the Church as it had been for centuries. Added to that, description in stories was usually extremely important so the reader or listener could build a detailed picture in their mind. Today many of us have so much information around us from the time we are born that just a key word would trigger a great deal of detail and imagery in the mind. That wasn't the case in the past.

Chapter 12

When Adam and Eve were expelled they had some knowledge unknown to the evolved humans but they were now amongst them. They passed on down to their family the knowledge of God creating our solar system and the Lord God who was in Eden by word of mouth. When their descendants became too influenced by the beliefs and traditions of "outsiders", "evolved humans" or gentiles, prophets and leaders came to try and put them back on track. However with any story over time there are subtle changes and this happened too with what became the Bible. That's why the Church wanted to canonise it so that no more changes could be made. However this caused problems as language and meanings of words change over time.

The knowledge Adam and Eve passed on was what they remembered regarding creation and what they wanted to pass on regarding themselves. Although disgraced at first they were honest enough to admit it and their descendants continued to pass on the key information as they remembered it. How the earth and planets came about and how there is a Creator who made our world and everything in it and how they should eat as a vegan then how it was modified after the Flood. Although their descendants initially became a polytheistic pastoralist social group this God became extremely important to them after Abraham led the way and later their descendants became the Jewish race.

Although the Flood spoken of in the Bible was something that affected Noah's area only there are many historical stories across the world of floods killing large numbers of people and animals as well as devastating land but scientifically found to be at different time periods from each other.

Obviously the telling of the creation of our world and solar system was done in an extremely simple way but it is basically scientifically correct and today it is realised the health benefits of a vegan diet to us and planet earth. To have had this information passed down to us from about 4,000 B.C.E. as intact as it is by word of mouth for generation after generation by people who hadn't scientific understanding as we know it, is amazing and thought provoking.

Acknowledgements

It has been suggested that I add a Bibliography to this to make the book more academic. However it would be difficult to do because this is a work that has evolved over many years through my understanding of the Bible, general learning and a Degree in Theology and Philosophy. Questions I've had since my teen years lingered, but over time, applying knowledge gained from other disciplines, for example etymology (the study of the history of words) and physics, I've come to conclusions that are written here. That said, there were sources that I used specifically which gave greater clarity for what I wanted. I needed to learn more about the history of the Devil and found from National Geographic's Documentary Tube "Devil's Bible" an author called Peter Stanford who wrote "The Devil: A Biography", which in turn showed me that the Hebrew for serpent could mean adversary which led me to look at early Hebrew pictographic writing. Additionally NASA's website NASA.gov gives a great deal of information about space. Finally I confirmed dates with encyclopaedias.

Out of the Darkness

The Theory of Everything

Introduction

There are many *"why's"*, *"what's"* and *"how's"* people ask to try and understand this world. Scientists can take these questions to work with them. It is their job to attempt to systematically understand our world and the universe we live in.

Historically theology tried to do the same. The chief difference is that while science questions, theology rests on a foundation of stories believed to be explanations of how the world, the universe and mankind were created. The information was taken as divine truth and was passed down with faithfulness because of fear of getting it wrong. It was not questioned because people were taught not to question God and centuries passed before any discoveries were made that would challenge the theological conception. The church taught that acceptance was the key to understanding and suffering was mankind's lot. It was mankind's fault because of original sin, the fall from grace for disobedience to God's command to not eat the fruit from the tree of knowledge of good and evil.

Because the Jews, and later the Christians due to their Jewish heritage, took the Creation stories as truth and therefore fact, it was extremely difficult and dangerous for Christians to question the stories because of the authority of the Church. This applied especially when evidence from scientific studies conflicted with biblical stories or the theological interpretation of the Bible. According to the Church the Bible could not be wrong because it was God's word, and its foundation had the weight of millennia of belief. And just as Galileo was persecuted in 1633 by the Inquisition for restating that Copernicus was right to believe that the Sun and not our Earth was the centre of this universe, the 1800's were full of serious conflicts between the Church and various scientists because scientific knowledge was increasing exponentially. One of the issues was started by Charles Darwin's theory of "natural selection" as the origins of human life on Earth. Another was the discovery of ever more dinosaur bones which started to be understood in a way that also conflicted with the established belief of the Church. However, there were also discoveries of other ancient Creation Stories like "The Epic of Gilgamesh" which the Church believed supported its belief in the Genesis story and the flood Noah and his family survived.

In the West both science and theology had had the same starting point - the Creation story from Genesis, and when the Church allowed, since it controlled education until comparatively recently, filtered down, censured classical philosophy. Philosophy also challenged Christianity. Not only had some classical philosophers tried to formulate the creation of our world and the universe but it was different from the Church's belief in Adam and Eve.

Additionally, the ancient Greeks were nominally polytheists. Despite this, some Greek philosophy was used by the Church to explain phenomena that developed within the Church like the Trinity. Also, despite what the Church said, the great classical thinkers as well as many of the Greek people, especially those who had had an education, had moved on from the pantheon of gods. They realised there was a supreme power which could not be defined except in abstract which they termed *"Logos"* or *"The One"*. Famously, St John, at the beginning of his gospel, used logos translated in King James' Bible as *"Word"*, which he linked to Jesus.

"In the beginning was the Word, and the Word was with God, and the Word was God."

Arabic culture had been more open to classical philosophy, even when it became Islamic, and it is in Arabic translations that much philosophy, especially Aristotle, was reclaimed by the West. Islam acknowledges the Genesis Creation Stories but has not emphasised them in the same way as Christianity. Also, Islam did not feel threatened by science so actively encouraged all branches of science including medicine. Yet western scientists, to exist and carry on much of their work, had to pursue and study it outside religion and at times in secret in fear of their lives because the Church was part of the Establishment. Science in the West became separated from the Church and its teachings, with the Church emphasising passages from the Bible such as,

"All scripture is inspired by God and is useful for teaching the truth, rebuking error, correcting faults and giving instruction for right living."

2 Timothy chapter 3, verse 16.

"Do not add anything to what I command you, and do not take anything away. Obey the commands of the Lord - -."

Deuteronomy chapter 4, verse 2.

"I, John, solemnly warn everyone who hears the prophetic words of this book: if anyone adds anything to them, God will add to his or her punishment the plagues described in this book. And if anyone takes anything away from the prophetic words of this book, God will take away from them their share of the fruit of the tree of life -."

Revelation chapter 22, verses 18 and 19.

However, despite these being used forcibly by the Church to squash any contradiction to its teaching, read in context, and with an open mind, they are not justifiably fully embracing. In other words, they do not prohibit new knowledge and understanding. The first quotation was to inspire spiritual awareness and understanding based on the Old Testament and the teaching of Jesus. The second, that from Deuteronomy chapter 4, relates to the Ten Commandments and the laws pertaining to the Jewish way of life. The third quotation, which comes from Revelation, refers to the Book of Revelation and not the whole Bible. The Book of Revelation was placed in the New Testament as its last Book, and the quotation is from the end of the last chapter of that book, so the quotation is also at the end of the whole Bible. It is in this position that it has been very forcibly used against people who question the authority of the Bible.

Many people lack interest in the Bible now, not only because they think of the creation stories, especially that of Adam and Eve, as fanciful, but also find it hard to believe in a God when there is so much suffering and injustice in the world. This has been compounded by the Church's historical attitude. Lack of interest leads to lack of knowledge

"Most cosmologists naturally want to find an all-embracing description of the universe within the laws of physics."

"Stephen Hawking's Universe, The Cosmos Explained" page 321.

In other words, they want to find a relationship between quantum mechanics (the science of everything smaller than an atom) and general relativity (the science of everything larger than an atom). This would be considered the Theory of Everything.

Every subject, discipline or career field uses specialised language. Those who do not know or use it are "outsiders". However, by not being able to use a certain specialised language does not necessarily mean that you are not capable of understanding a subject, discipline or career field. It is like going to a foreign country which has an unknown language, but items of food are familiar although the method of cooking them and the presentation may be different.

Because religion has existed for millennia, and to at least some extent, is still a subject that encompasses many people, there are religious words that are universally understood whether one is an atheist (outsider) or not. There are also accepted religious doctrines, which are really religious theories, that are known by atheists as well as those who believe in them.

Science attempts to systematically understand our world and the universe we live in. Theology had tried to do the same. The trouble was that when scientific discoveries showed that life and the world were different from what the church taught there was conflict. The conflict escalated as more was discovered that was at variance with the church's doctrines, (theories). Scientists had to work in secret and science became a discipline outside the church. Theology renounced science and science denied theology. A serious rift began, each discipline with its own theories.

The concepts accepted by religion are not quantifiable in conventional or classical scientific terms. As a result, it is commonly accepted that science and religion are two disciplines not able to easily reconcile.

However, in the twentieth century, physics began to use new kinds of mathematical models to describe the universe. These models employed imaginary numbers and had nothing to do with the real world, that is, the world as commonly understood by humans. Despite this, there are effects that have been predicted correctly and other effects that have been observed, although they have not been able to be measured, so are believed by scientists to be there.

In theology, the language of religion, there are

effects that have been observed. These include such events as Moses leading the Children of Israel from Egypt, Exodus chapter 14, and Moses bringing the Ten Commandments down from Mount Sinai, Exodus chapter 19. The birth of Jesus is documented in St Luke chapter 2 verses 1 to 18 and the teaching and miracles he performed in his adult life are reported in all four Gospels. Mohammed's life (pbuh) and dictating of the Qur'an are chronicled in Islam. Although none of these events have been measured scientifically, they have been observed, recorded, and subsequently devoutly believed by religious people. But then there are effects like God, the Creation and an afterlife that have not been measured but are believed to exist by religious people.

Stephen Hawking believed that science should be able to explain all aspects of the universe if its theories are correct. This thinking is unusual among scientists. Most either avoid confrontation about the beginning of the world or maintain that religion or metaphysics should deal with it.

Science and mathematics are generally considered precise disciplines. Physics, a branch of science, uses mathematics to calculate its findings but it does not always offer a straightforward answer. This has been especially since the discovery of, and within the field of quantum mechanics, (subatomic physics).

"All measurements (of elementary particles and forces) involve disentangling things that can't be separated, or quantifying things that can't be counted, or defining things that you can't quite put your finger on. Usually, the act of measuring something affects it; sometimes measurement destroys it."

"The Universe and the Teacup", page 42. Also,

"Subatomic particles cannot be precisely measured without making quantifiable sacrifices. If you measure precisely what a particle is doing, you cannot at the same time measure precisely where it is. If you measure precisely how much energy it has, you lose all information about time."

Ibid, page 44.

And very importantly, a quote from page 46 of the same book,

"Perhaps the most insidious obstacle to accurate measurement is the normally unacknowledged fact that you can only measure the stuff that you go out and look for, stuff that you know (or suspect) is actually there."

Belief motivated Abbe Georges Lemaitre to find proof that the universe was finite and therefore created. Lemaitre was a Jesuit priest and the leading theoretical cosmologist working at the Vatican Observatory. By using Einstein's mathematics but removing the constant that

Einstein had inserted, Lemaitre showed that the universe was dynamic and not static as proposed by Isaac Newton. In 1931 he first put forward the theory of a gently expanding universe and a *"primeval atom"*. Lemaitre believed that he had shown scientific evidence that the universe had been created *"on a day that had no yesterday"* which supported the biblical idea of creation. After initial rejection, this not only won Einstein's sincere approval and acceptance, but Einstein acknowledged that the constant he had inserted was the greatest mistake of his life.

Lemaitre had opponents who supported a different theory which they called the "Steady State Theory". In the 1940's one of them called Fred Hoyle, when ridiculing the "Primeval Atom Theory" coined the expression *"Big Bang"* to describe it. However, subsequently, there has been increasing evidence to support the "Big Bang".

Other theorists following Einstein's maths of relativity pursued different implications. As a result, Roger Penrose deduced what he called *"a point of singularity"*. Later this became known as a *"black hole"*. It was Stephen Hawking who could see that the primeval atom or Big Bang was the reversal of a point of singularity or black hole. Stephen Hawking did work which supported this theory but also called the primeval atom *"a singularity"*. His work was one of the pieces of evidence that supported the Big Bang theory.

The central problem to finding the Theory of Everything is the mismatch between the physics of everything larger than an atom (relativity) and the physics of everything smaller than an atom (quantum mechanics). Einstein's Theory of General Relativity explains what is larger than an atom, that is, the dynamics of the universe. Anything smaller than an atom is described by Heisenberg's Uncertainty Principle and Schrodinger's formulated idea of wave particle duality. However, physicists have not been able to connect the two areas of physics at the point where they believe they should meet.

"The large physics of the universe (governed by gravity, and springing from a tiny singularity) needs to embrace the small physics of quantum mechanics in order to explain how that singularity can arise and give birth to the Big Bang and the gravitational effects which shape the universe from it".

"Stephen Hawking's Universe, the Cosmos Explained", pages 231 and 232.

The criterion for finding the Theory of Everything for science, specifically for physics, is therefore to find something that fully embraces the theories of relativity with those of quantum mechanics. To theology, God is the answer and what has not been answered by knowledge has had to be accepted by faith. Additionally, as has been stated, it is necessary to know, or believe you know, what you are looking for, to have any chance of finding it.

I believe in God. I believe he is real, exists and is the Creator. I also believe in life after death. Not only that, but I also believe that what is called God is the "Theory of Everything". To prove my theory, I will use fundamental laws and principles of physics to explain my belief. And remember, what Shakespeare said through Juliet in his play Romeo and Juliet, *"A rose by any other name would smell as sweet."* (Act 2 scene 2) I add that a name is a label.

Part 1

"For anything to happen, energy is needed, and when anything happens energy is converted from one form to another."

"Energy can take many different forms - - for example, heat, light and sound as well as chemical, kinetic and potential."

"Energy cannot be created or destroyed. It can only be changed into a different form."

There are energy chains and

"An energy chain is a way of showing how energy is converted from one form to another."

(The Usborne Internet-Linked Library of Science Energy, Forces and Motion)

In other words, everything stems from energy. Energy came first, it was before anything else, and it is the source of everything in the universe. Energy cannot die, instead it manifests in different ways. Each time it forms something new, it creates. When to human perception one form dies it is really the result of that expression of energy becoming unsustainable. The energy then takes on another guise, but it cannot cease to exist. It progresses through energy chains. Additionally, some forms of energy are invisible to us.

"Once created, things work towards disintegration."

"The Universe in a Nutshell" page 97.

"The only time that exists is the atoms own internal clock - the frequency at which it vibrates. But put a bunch of atoms together, and no one has any problem telling which way time flows: It's always in the direction of disorder. Left to its own devices, food rots, skin wrinkles, paint peels, mountains erode, stockings run."

"The Universe and the Teacup" page 64.

Thermodynamics, a branch of science, qualifies the statement about energy not being created or destroyed,

*"In **a closed system** energy may change form but cannot be created or destroyed".*

Stephen Hawking proposes a *"no boundary universe"* but of finite size. "Stephen Hawking's Universe, The Cosmos Explained" page 247. This would mean that the universe does not have a specific shape or size but also that space or time has no end. Conversely, if space and time have no end, they have no beginning either. This is "*a closed system*". However, a beginning was proposed by Lemaitre, and Hawking believes Lemaitre's theory is viable despite it not being able to fit within the laws of physics as they are currently understood.

"All life relies on chemical reactions."

Paul Davis in "About Time" quoted on page 58 of "The Universe and the Teacup".

But while all life relies on chemical reactions, chemical reactions rely on energy. As previously stated, everything relies on energy both initially, and subsequently, it is a universal constant. It is the form energy takes that varies according to circumstance.

Energy is within every cell of everything at sub-atomic level. It remains in everything at atomic level. It also manifests itself cosmically.

String theory, a relatively new branch of physics, acknowledges this and considers energy could be the unifying factor of the Theory of Everything.

Energy itself is not possible to define though. The actions and reactions of energy are. The following is taken from a paper written by Dr Richard Feynman entitled *"What is Energy?"*. It can be found on: http//physics.cusm.edu/201/ Resour...EnergyQuote. pdf

"It is important to realise in physics today, we have no knowledge of what energy is. We do not have a picture that energy comes in little blobs of a definite amount. It is not that way. However, there are formulas for calculating some numerical quality, and

when we add it all together, it gives "28" - always the same number. It is an abstract thing in that it does not tell us the mechanisms or reasons for the various formulas."

According to physics, energy creates, destroys, and is the power behind everything. There is even energy in apparently empty space currently defined as *"vacuum energy"*. "The Universe in a Nutshell" page 96. But still no one knows what energy looks like behind all its various manifestations. Although String Theory gets the closest to analysing it, even to that specialised branch of physics "energy" still "just is".

"I am that I am," said God to Moses from a bush that was in flames but did not burn. Exodus chapter 3, verse 14. The anthropomorphic God exhibited earlier in the Bible, in Genesis, has metamorphosed. God, in the form humans were supposed to be made in the image of, as shown in Genesis chapters 1 and 2, has changed appearance. To those who believe in God, He can express Himself in any way. He is the power behind the universe and some intangible *"Being"* they pray to.

Also, from a theological standpoint God creates, just as science speaks of energy doing. Theology frequently links both creation and power to God. Some people believe God is also capable of destroying. The definition of *"power"* in science is the rate energy is produced or used. No one on earth knows what God looks like but those who believe in Him consider He is the creator of this world, the universe and all that is living – the unseen power. They believe He manifests in different ways and speaks through human beings who become known as prophets or, in the case of Jesus to Christians, His Son.

The following is a small but relevant selection of biblical references.

"- - hast though not heard, that the everlasting God, the Lord, the Creator of the ends of the earth, fainteth not, neither is weary? - - He giveth power to the faint - -."
Isaiah chapter 40, verse 28.

"- - power belongeth unto God."
 Psalm 62 verse 11.

"God is my strength and power - -."
2 Samuel chapter 22 verse 33.

"- - they were all amazed at the mighty power of God"
(as shown through Jesus*).*
Luke chapter 9, verse 43.

And in the Lord's Prayer, Matthew chapter 6, verse 13,

" - - for thine is the kingdom, the power and the glory, - -."

Part 2

"In the beginning God (energy) *created the heaven and the earth."*
Genesis chapter 1, verse 1.

Then is listed the order things were created. This is basic but has been shown to be close to scientifically correct despite being written before there was a scientific explanation for anything. The Bible continues,
"Thus, the heavens and the earth were finished and all the host of them."
Genesis chapter 2, verse 1.

Here, it seems to say that while there was one earth, there were many heavens. In fact, there are many heavens or *"solar systems"* according to science.

As stated earlier, Stephen Hawking proposed a no boundary universe. It has also been accepted that there could have been a beginning to the universe, and that if it did, as Lemaitre's theory goes, our universe was created. Stephen Hawking and others find Lemaitre's theory not only plausible and consistent with Einstein's maths, but Hawking had also proposed that Roger Penrose's theory of singularities (black holes) was the inverse of the primeval atom theory. So, he says, if Lemaitre's theory is correct so would Penrose's be. Subsequently black holes (singularities) have been studied and found to be in the plural. They have also been found to have existed historically. I would therefore suggest that Lemaitre's theory should be understood as our solar system "universe" coming into existence that way within the "greater universe" or the whole cosmos because every universe within the whole cosmos could have begun in that same way, but at different times. Lemaitre's theory implies one primeval atom at the beginning of time. Stephen Hawking's proposition of "a no boundary universe" can be contemplated with these theories because black holes and inflation theory go together. That is because the part of the universe surrounding a black hole expands in readiness to accommodate what comes out of the black hole's inversion as the Big Bang. The universe begins to expand once a black hole has reached a certain size. It's just like a spot or boil forming on the skin. The skin around it swells. It does not mean that the whole body has swollen. Although inflation theory can accommodate Lemaitre's theory, which in turn accommodates black holes, inflation theory was proposed for a different reason. It is because time and space are synonymous in physics and because they are understood this way they can accommodate inflation theory.

In his more recent book, "The Universe in a Nutshell" Stephen Hawking states in chapter 3 that if, as he and Hartle proposed, the histories of the universe were indeed closed surfaces, then the universe would be self-contained. This is also consistent with a no boundary universe and can also accommodate Feynman's multiple histories theory and that black holes invert becoming "white holes", another theory. So, if the universe has no boundary and is therefore self-contained I suggest that everything within it must be recycled. It would need to be. I also suggest that that is at least part of the purpose of energy chains. On a universal scale that is what black holes do when they gravitationally pull into themselves anything within their gravitational influence, or when a large dying star becomes a black hole. This is because when a black hole is full, it bursts open or explodes creating the Big Bang and out pours everything it has taken in but in the form of refined elements, as known in the Periodic Table. These are the basic building blocks of life and life is starting over again. There is complete regeneration. The change happens because of the intense heat within the black hole. Those elements create a new planet, planetary system or universe depending on the size of the black hole and therefore the amount that comes out.

An example of natural recycling on earth is the leaves falling from trees in the autumn and breaking down to create humus, nutrition for the soil. If nature did not recycle or regenerate itself the universe could not survive. On every level, from stars to humans to insects, things wear out or die then change their form of existence and continue in their energy chains. Humans who believe theology believe that when they die to this world their spirit (what had been their embodied energy) will pass on to another existence. Depending on the religion they acknowledge, they believe they will go to heaven, paradise or hell; or be reincarnated. Energy does not cease to exist, it changes form. Humans are part of life therefore part of the energy chain. They are not exempt from wearing out; the process is just euphemised as *"getting old"*.

Part 3

The intense heat at the moment of collision in a particle accelerator simulating the Big Bang produces only pure energy initially. This energy is pure light and has no electrical charge. After that, when there has been some cooling, particles of matter and antimatter appear. "Stephen Hawking's Universe, The Universe Explained" page 146.

Matter and antimatter could also be known as positive and negative energies.

Theologically pure light is the first expression of creation, the first thing that separates.

Genesis chapter 1, verse 1
"In the beginning God created the heaven and the earth. And the earth was without form and void - -. And the spirit of God (pure energy) *moved upon the face of the waters.* (NASA has found water in space around a huge black hole it is monitoring) *and God said let there be light, and there was light."*

As said the Big Bang produces only pure energy initially which manifests as pure light. It has no electric charge and is balanced within itself.

"- -and God saw the light, that is was good, and God divided the light from the darkness".

Genesis chapter 1 verse 4.

(It then became matter and antimatter)

A new universe or solar system was born out of the contents ejected from a black hole and God is the creative energy. This was not Earth's day and night being created because the sun and moon were not created until verse 16 of Genesis chapter 1.

I put forward that there is an even bigger consideration now. If singularities or the Big Bang emerge from black holes, how can a singularity have come first and on its own? Surely that supports the no boundary universe theory. It also shows that energy (God the Creator) came before it. Remember a name is a label however revered that name becomes. And science and religion are different disciplines, historically estranged but both wanting the ultimate answer.

The four forces of nature accepted by physics, the strong, the electromagnetic, the weak and the gravitational are all expressions of energy. Surely energy is their common denominator, the "Theory of Everything".

Energy and mass (matter) are interchangeable and always directly proportional. "Stephen Hawking's Universe, the Cosmos Explained" page 141. (God is in everything – omnipresent)

Energy is fundamental to all matter.
Ibid page142.

(Without God nothing could be created)
"- the Lord God made the earth and the heavens,- ".
Genesis chapter 2 verse 4

Only energy can exist in the immense temperature of the black hole and the initial burst of the Big Bang. Conversely in the microscopic world, energy causes subatomic particles, (electrons, negative charge) and their anti-particles, (positrons, positive charge), to collide. On collision there is a burst of energy that creates a photon (single light particle). This releases energy to produce other electron and positron pairs. "The Universe in a Nutshell" page 51. (This is creation!) The matter and antimatter that emerges from the pure light energy attracts, collides, and mimicking the Big Bang's explosion, reforms. Anti-matter disappears when it reacts with other particles, frequently fractions of a second after being created.

I put forward that in a theological sense this is the initial stage of "good" and "bad" fighting and forming. The fight continues through the process of creation to the created being influenced and continues throughout development and life.

"No man hath seen God (pure energy) *at any time. If we love one another, God dwelleth in us* (pure/good energy) *and his love is perfected in us."*

I John verse 12

According to an unproven theory, the slight excess of matter left intact after the collisions of particles and antiparticles could have formed everything in the universe. This is consistent with Einstein's maths. Ibid page 148. It also fits theologically. We have God and His creation.

"Hereby we know that we dwell in him, and he in us, because he hath given us of his spirit. (energy)*"*

1 John verse 13

I also put forward that energy strives to maintain its balance of neutral, positive and negative throughout all of existence from subatomic level upwards. Once things are created "natural selection" and "natural disasters" like volcanoes, earthquakes, tornadoes, and tsunamis continue the process. Going even bigger, so do Black Holes.

According to science energy and mass are interchangeable and always directly proportional. In Isaiah chapter 45, verse 7, God is quoted as saying,

"I create both light and darkness; I bring both blessing and disaster. I, the Lord do all these things."

Taken from the Good News Bible.

If God is the power of creation or energy of

creation He can be understood this way. However, an evil force separate from God has been acknowledged since "the days of Adam and Eve" and it has been believed that it can be fed by more evil.

A destructive energy, an excess of negative energy, is really an imbalance within the whole system, and will be destroyed sooner or later. This is because the imbalance in energy causes further imbalance, and further imbalance causes destruction. The difference between destruction and decay is that destruction is forced regeneration by violent means brought about from energy outside the organism being destroyed while decay is a link in the chain of natural or non-invasive regeneration. Decay is a continual and comparatively gentle process that is part of the organism's life pattern, the process of "getting old".

As stated before, when to human perception one form dies, it is really the result of that expression of energy becoming unsustainable. The energy then takes on other guises, but it cannot cease to exist. Death is purely the end of one life or one form of existence and the beginning of the next in an energy chain. Some forms of energy are invisible to us but,

"Energy cannot be created or destroyed. It can only be changed into a different form."

"The Usbourne Internet-Linked Library of Science. Energy, Forces and Motion".

"Once created, things work towards disintegration."

"The Universe in a Nutshell" Page 97. And

"The only time that exists is the atom's own internal clock - the frequency at which it vibrates. But put a bunch of atoms together, and no one has any problem telling which way time flows: It's always in the direction of disorder."

"The Universe and the Teacup" page 64.
Theology states that when people die they pass on to a different life, a spiritual existence. It is their energy which is their life-force that is their soul/spirit. It leaves their body when their physical body is no longer able to sustain it. It then goes on to the next step in the energy chain. All the mainstream religions teach that life does not cease to exist with earthly death just as physics maintains that energy and mass (matter) are interchangeable and always directly proportional and that not all forms are visible. So as thoughts and actions are also expressions of energy, the amount of good and bad energies that a person has expressed throughout their life is also accountable or measured, just as theology teaches that our souls (the energy force that kept our earthly body alive) are weighed to show how good or bad we have been. The energy (or soul or spirit) which is really who or what we are, is our

own energy embodiment from conception and birth to this life, transformed or metamorphosed during life by how we have lived and expressed ourselves, since thoughts, words and deeds are forms of energy. But we are not pure energy: we are a mixture of good and bad energy. The way we lead our lives raises or lowers our energy status quo.

Jesus speaks about evil at different times and in different ways. One time, after he was praised by a watching crowd who saw him heal a deaf and dumb man who was said to have a devil in him because he was deaf and dumb, members of a different sect who had also been onlookers in the crowd accused him of making the man better through Beelzebub, the prince of devils. Jesus' reply was,

"Every kingdom divided against itself is brought to desolation; and every city or house divided against itself shall not stand - - if Satan cast out Satan, he is divided against himself - -."

Gospel of St Matthew, chapter 12, verses 25 and 26 and the Gospel of St Luke chapter 18 verses 18 – 23.

He also said,

"To have good fruit you must have a healthy tree; if you have a poor tree, you will have bad fruit. A tree is known by the fruit it bears"

Gospel of St Matthew, verse 33. Then continuing: -

"For the heart speaks what the heart is full of. A good person brings good things out of a treasure of good things; a bad person brings bad things out of a treasure of bad things."

Ibid verses 34 and 35.

Continuing, Jesus says,

"You can be sure that on Judgement Day everyone will have to give account of every useless word he has ever spoken. Your words will be used to judge you – to declare you either innocent or guilty."

Part 4

"When it comes to sub-atomic chemical reactions Werner Heisenberg's Uncertainty Principle states that it is impossible to pinpoint both the momentum of a particle and its position at the same time. You simply cannot know how a particle is behaving - you have to accept the uncertainty of the situation - and this must include such improbable sounding events as particles popping in and out of existence".

"The Universe and the Teacup" page 207.

"Unpredictability does not mean that subatomic behaviour does not have causes; it only means that it has causes too subtle and complex for us to untangle."
(I add, - with our current knowledge)

Ibid, page 131.

Quotation from the Born Einstein correspondence contained in Born's "The Natural Philosophy of Cause and Chance".
"a single particle can go backwards and forwards in space or time"

Ibid, page 64.

According to Einstein *"Time and space are mathematically one and the same thing."*
Stephen Hawking's Universe, The Cosmos Explained" page 83.

"Time as we know it, is a man-made construct to give us greater definition and understanding to our existence."

"From molecule size matter, electrical forces take over; scale up further and gravity rules. - -Add more matter and the squeeze of gravity ignites nuclear fires. Stars exist in a continual tug of war between gravitational collapse and the outward pressure of nuclear fire - over time gravity wins and a giant star collapses and becomes a black hole – anything can be a black hole."

"The Universe and the Teacup" page 57.

Then from page 63,

"Something comes into being on the scale of many that does not exist on the scale of few - e.g. a single water molecule cannot freeze or a single carbon atom cannot have the hardness or sparkle of a diamond".

I suggest that the unpredictability of the sub-atomic is not only the energy within trying to become definitive, but the balance of potential positive (good/strong) and negative (bad/weak) energy forming itself, creating an electric current in the process. The electric current being its "life force", i.e. its "energy"

From molecule size upwards this has been achieved but the process of growth and definition continues. Whatever it is to become, more molecules are attracted and its expression achieves further definition whether it is a plant, tree, animal, fish or human. This is how it works.

Inside an atom (positively charged) is a nucleus and electrons (negatively charged). The electrons inside the atom orbit the nucleus. Inside the nucleus are protons (positively charged) and neutrons (no electric charge). The protons and neutrons within an atom have the same weight. The protons and electrons have similar magnitude but opposite charge.

However, if the balance within the atom is upset/ changed by gaining or losing electrons the electrical charge which was in balance becomes an electrical current. When this happens, electrons move from one atom to another. It does not affect the nuclei though.

Everything at its most basic is a form of energy. The physical / scientific explanation above describes simply how everything is composed on an atomic level, and how it both is, and can be affected by, energy. Specific atomic composition determines what something is and what we recognize it as. Examples are sodium (salt), gold, lead, oxygen and water. More complex types of definition are genetic. Examples are people and other land animals, birds and sea creatures, trees and plants. These are not only made up of atoms to create something recognizable for example a boy or woman, dog or cat, a daffodil or an oak tree, but there is genetic variation to a greater or lesser degree within each specific type.

Since everything is an expression of energy it follows that everything is potentially capable of being affected by the electrical current that pulses through energy. Things can be affected a little or a lot, directly or indirectly, but to an immediate or delayed extent, everything is affected. People, creatures and nature in general are affected by weather conditions – forms of energy, and nutrition, another form of energy, as well as by thoughts and emotions, again, forms of energy. Although people understand plants are affected by weather conditions and nutrition (good or bad soil) scientists have shown that they, just like creatures and us humans, are affected by vibrations of energy, even from a distance. These includes feelings sent out from people as well as sounds, - voices, music and industrial machinery. Sound = electric currents = energy. Creature and plant responses may be simpler, but they exist. Human responses are more complex that is all.

Each of us humans, similar to creatures and plants, are a specific composition of atoms. The atoms are self-contained microscopic "balls" of electrical energy which are held together by the energy that creates us and them. It defines us and them so we are recognizable. A friend, a dog or fish, a flower or tree and so on. Good health makes the atoms vibrant while poor health makes them weak. A change in the energy flow – the electrical current – in anything alive – makes changes in the person, creature or plant.

Now to speak specifically about humans. A change in our disposition also changes the electrical flow because our disposition is the energy we are creating within and pouring out. There are those who can see auras, which are really the electrical energy flowing around living things, and those who are *"sensitive"* who see or feel the change even if it is small. If there is a big change, for example great happiness or enthusiasm, great sadness or anger, the change is obvious to almost everyone without seeing an aura. The greater the change of emotion, the greater the agitation of the atoms composing the person. If the electrical energy within the atoms increases to a certain level it becomes an electric current which attracts or repels. Because of this, emotions like falling in love or great hate affects other humans and creatures around us. Also large gatherings of people can be manipulated. Character or temperament change occurs when the influence is strong or permanent. In this way people are influenced and influence others. They can be influenced for the better or worse, that is good or bad. The vibrations (energy) they send out attracts whatever energy responds to it. Anything and everything around humans can influence them. Advertising preys on and makes money from that fact. But as religion warns us theologically, our conscience is affected by good or bad, that is, it either works positively or negatively.

There are religious paintings that show halos around the heads of characters considered sacred. Halos are part of the aura. Many were painted centuries ago which is interesting.

Scientifically, all objects emit radiation (heat) that spans a spectrum of frequencies. This is another way of expressing, interpreting or understanding electrical energy. As the heat increases so does frequency (movement). The amount of energy radiated (poured out) increases with frequency and so does the temperature because the atoms move faster and faster so get increasingly hot. That is what happens when someone gets agitated and also how "vibes" pass between people. It is also the aura in action. Electrical energy is transmitted through vibration. Being neutral is when the atoms are not disturbed sufficiently to make them lose or gain electrons. In other words, they are not open to being influenced or affected by what is around them on an atomic level or a human level. An electron in its orbit within its nucleus can remain neutral indefinitely without using or losing energy. Buddhists aim to follow the *"middle way"* which is being undisturbed by excessive emotion or effects outside oneself.

Part 5

Light rays cause some substances to give up electrons and produce an electric current (photovoltaic effect), but a beam of pure light energy has no electrical charge, in other words it is neutral or balanced within itself. "Stephen Hawking's Universe the Cosmos Explained" page 146.

Jesus is quoted as saying in the Gospel of St John, chapter 8 verse 12,

"I am the light of the world: he that followeth me shall not walk in darkness, but shall have the light of life."

Jesus was speaking metaphorically but the metaphor also has a deeper and profound meaning if the scientific understanding is attached to it.

That is, understanding that the pure energy produced at the moment of creation, the Big Bang, is pure light and has no electrical charge. Also, that energy and mass are interchangeable and always directly proportional.

On the first level of understanding, the theological, the teaching of Jesus can have a good influence on people. Good vibrations are created and passed on which affect change for the better or reinforce the good that was already there. On the second level, the scientific, the spirit of Jesus is embodied pure light energy. (Energy and mass are interchangeable) Also, He is saying that we can be the same if we follow his teaching summarized as,

"Thou shalt love the Lord thy God with all thy heart, and with all thy soul, and with all thy mind" and secondly,

"Thou shalt love thy neighbour as thyself."

The first part of the summary is actually taken from part of the Shema; the Shema being the most important part of the Jewish morning and evening prayers. Jesus was Jewish. The very first "Christians" were a sect of Judaism. This part of the Shema was taken from Chapter 6 verse 5 of the Book of Deuteronomy in the Old Testament of the Christian Bible which copied the book of Deuteronomy in the Jewish Torah.

Jesus added that if we really did follow these words there would be no need for other laws or commandments.

This is recorded in the Gospels of Mathew 22 verses 35-40, Mark 12 verses 28-34 and Luke 10 verse 27.

Theologically Jesus is believed to have been with God when the world began and after his earthly death it was accepted that Jesus returned to be one with God. In other words, He is part of the energy of creation we know as God. By theological descriptions Jesus is synonymous with the pure light energy that is the first energy to burst out at the moment of the creation of our universe. This was shown graphically when he was, in Christian terminology, "Transfigured". The story is told in the Gospels of Matthew, Mark and Luke of how he took his three closest disciples, Peter, James and John up a mountain to a secluded place and showed himself to them as pure spirit with Moses and Elijah, the two majorly important figures in Judaism who had died many years previously. Moses had given them (the Jews) their Law and Elijah was considered their greatest prophet. Symbolically this meant Jesus was the fulfilment of the law and the prophets. (This was referring to the Jewish Law, the laws pertaining to the Jewish way of life)

Matthew 17 verses 1–8, Mark 9 verses 2–8 and Luke 9 verse 28–36.

The Gospel of St John in chapter 16 verses 27 and 28 quotes Jesus as saying,

"For the Father himself loveth you, because ye have loved me, and have believed that I came out from God.
I came forth from the Father, and am come into the world: again, I leave the world, and go to the Father."

(God as Creation and Jesus coming from the pure light that came first from the Big Bang)
There is no death: life or light, manifestations of energy, go on existing. The better the person the

purer the energy or light coming from them. Jesus' spirit is pure light energy and He told the people listening to Him that if they followed how He told them to live they could be too. When He spoke the Sermon on the Mount,

" Ye (you) are the light of the world - - - - -Let your light so shine before men that they may see your good works, and glorify your Father who is in heaven." *(Matthew 5: 14 -16)*

And in St John chapter 8 verse 24 Jesus is in the middle of an argument with some Jews.

"Jesus said unto them, If God were your Father, (which refers to the creation story in Genesis where God creates Adam and Eve) *you would love me: for I proceeded forth and came from God: neither came I of myself, but he sent me."*

Jesus came from the pure light energy of the creation of our universe.

Also, in chapter 8, but in verse 58 Jesus says,

"Before Abraham was, I am." Jesus existed before Abraham and continues to live ("I am" speaking in the present).

This is reminiscent of God talking to Moses through the bush that burned but was not consumed by the fire when God said,
"I am, that I am."

The Jews would be familiar with the Moses story and immediately understand the link.

Then in St John chapter 17 verses 4 and 5, Jesus is quoted as praying to God in the Garden of Gethsemane, on the eve of his death, as follows,

"I have glorified thee on the earth: I have finished the work which thou gavest me to do.
And now, O Father, glorify thou me with thy own self with the glory which I had with thee before the world was."

Scientifically pure light energy comes first from the pure energy of a Big Bang. Then it is followed by the elements that form the new solar system. **Energy and mass are interchangeable.**

Colossians chapter 1 verses 16 to 19.
"For by him were all things created, that are in heaven, and that are in the earth, visible and invisible, - -, all things were created by him and for him:
and he is before all things, and by him all things consist. - - .
For it pleased the Father that in him should all fullness dwell."

There are several references to Jesus being called the Son of God in the New Testament from his birth recorded in St Matthew and St Luke, and his baptism also in St Matthew and St Luke to his temptation by Satan in St Matthew and St Luke.

He was also the Son of God in a scientific sense.

The Creed, which is the statement of belief recited by communicants in both the Roman Catholic and Church of England churches, states that Jesus is the only begotten Son of God.

"I believe in one God the Father Almighty, Maker of heaven and earth, And of all things visible and invisible:
And in one Lord Jesus Christ, the only-begotten Son of God, Begotten of his Father before all worlds, God of God, Light of Light, Very God of very God, Begotten, not made, Being of one substance with the Father, By whom all things were made: Who for us men and for our salvation came down from heaven - - -."

St John stated in chapter 3 verse 16,

"For God so loved the world that he gave his only begotten Son, that whosoever believeth in him should not perish, but have everlasting life."

Light produces an electric potential between layers of different substances. When light falls on an object the object either reflects it or absorbs it. Light is made up of the spectrum of colours of the rainbow. The colours that are NOT absorbed by an object are the colours the object is seen as. All colours and their shades vibrate at certain frequencies. The objects that reflect nearly all the light that falls on them appear white and objects that absorb nearly all the light that falls on them appear black.

"Eye Witness Science: Light and Lasers" page 35. "Stephen Hawking's Universe, The Cosmos Explained" page146.

"There are specific wavelengths of light, where each element either absorbs light, creating an absence of light, (or a dark line), or radiates light, creating a brighter colour or extra light. It is all to do with the sub-atomic structure of each element and the way it responds to the input of energy."

Ibid page 63.

Theologically it is accepted that we can radiate light or goodness ourselves. Jesus tells us in his Sermon on the Mount, St Matthew chapter 5 verse 16

"Let your light (your energy / spirit) so shine before men, that they may see your good works, and glorify your Father which is in heaven."

Equally we can do bad and be full of darkness.

"Woe unto them that call evil good, and good evil; that put darkness for light, and light for darkness;- - ".
Isaiah chapter 5 verse 20.

In St Matthew chapter 6 verses 22 and 23 is the following,

"The eyes are like a lamp for the body. If your eyes are sound, your whole body will be full of light; but if your eyes are no good, your body will be in darkness. So if the light in you is darkness, how terribly dark it will be."

Taken from the Good News Bible.

In other words, people who see the good, try to be good by following good. They know the difference between good and bad and try to shun the bad. By doing this they become a shining example for others or, as Jesus puts it, a light for others to follow. If one follows bad any light within will become darkness. In other words, the person will become worse unless there is some intervention.

CONCLUSION

"- - the ultimate explanation of the universe at its most microscopic level, a theory that does not rely on any deeper explanation - would provide the firmest foundation on which to build our understanding of the world. Its discovery would mark a beginning, not an end. The ultimate theory would provide an unshakeable pillar of coherence forever assuring us that the universe is a comprehensible place."

"The Elegant Universe" page 17.

"- even these paradigm-shaking discoveries (relating to what has been so far discovered in the field of string theory) *are only part of a larger, all-encompassing story. With solid faith that laws of the large and the small should fit together into a coherent whole, physicists are relentlessly hunting down the elusive unified theory. The search is not over - "*

Ibid, page 386.

My statement. Nothing exists without energy physically (scientifically), or without God, (theologically). Physics has shown that energy creates everything in existence, religion claims God is the Creator of everything. Both are invisible and without form yet take shape through manifestation. Energy cannot be destroyed and God is eternal. Energy is within everything, has ultimate control over everything, and knowledge within itself of everything, while theologically, God is omnipresent, omnipotent and omniscient.

Energy and God are different words to explain the same thing.

From this leads everything else.

Bibliography

Cole, K.C. : *The Universe and the Teacup,* Abacus, reprint 1999

Filkin, David : *Stephen Hawking's Universe, The Cosmos Explained,* BBC Books, 1997

Greene, Brian :*The Elegant Universe*, Jonathan Cape, London, UK, 1999

Hawking, Stephen : *The Universe in a Nutshell,* Bantam Press, 2001

Hess, Fred C. : *Chemistry Made Simple,* W. H. Allen and Company. Reprint 1967.

Kerrod, Robin: *Light and Lasers,* Oxford University Press, 1993

Parker, Steve: *Eye Witness Science, Electricity, In Association with The Science Museum London*, Dorling Kindersley, 1992.

The Oxford Companion to the Bible : edited by Bruce M Metzger and Michael D Coogan, Oxford University Press 1993.

The Usbourne Internet-Linked Library of Science. Energy, Forces and Motion. Usbourne Publishing Ltd., London EC1N 8RT, England

The Bible : Authorised King James version and Good News Bible, HarperCollins, second edition